Keto Diet for Dummies 2021

The Complete 2021 Keto Diet Cookbook |
Lose Weight, Burn Fat & Live Healthier With
Simple and Delicious Low-Carb Ketogenic
Recipes (14-Day Meal Plan Included)

Julia Spoon

Introduction

Congratulations on purchasing *Keto Diet for Dummies 2021,* the book you need to begin your keto lifestyle this year. This book outlines keto cooking and how you can start this new lifestyle in the New Year and turn your life around while doing so.

The New Year is a time for new beginnings, and there is nothing better than beginning the New Year with a fantastic lifestyle guaranteed to turn your life around. That is what the keto diet will do for you. It will give you the power you need to change your eating habits so you can completely transform your life. Keto eating is a healthy way to burn the excess fat in your body and turn it into energy. Your body will use fat for fuel instead of carbohydrates, breaking your dependence on processed foods and sugary foods. You will enable the ability to control your appetite, and you will lose the food cravings that keep you chained in that unhealthy body. And you will do all this while enjoying a surge in energy.

No matter what else is going on in your life, your health should be your number one priority. Keto is a lifestyle you will adopt, and not just a diet you will use for a short time and then abandon. You will remain keto no matter where you go or what you are doing. There will be adjustments to be made, and this is true with any lifestyle change. But when you change to keto, and your body accepts the adjustments you will make, you will find freedom with the food you never tried before. You will once again enjoy the food you eat without being tied to the habit of regularly eating.

Even though the keto diet has its restrictions, much like any other diet, there are so many foods you will enjoy eating that you will not miss the ones you can't have. The keto diet structure makes it easy to cook food in large batches for several days, eat, take food with you, or even eat out with friends and family. And you will not only lose weight, but you will find it easy to keep that excess weight from ever coming back.

Thank you for choosing *Keto Diet for Dummies 2021* out of the many choices available to you. Please enjoy the delicious recipes and useful information as you begin your extraordinary new journey.

Chapter 1: The Keto Diet

On the other side, a keto diet often contributes to ketosis, which will be consuming forever. Being on a keto, diet provides all of the advantages of fasting without needing to exercise long term, including weight reduction.

When You Are in Ketosis, How Would You Know?

To figure out if you are in a ketosis condition, search for ketones in your urine. You can order ketone strips digitally or from a local pharmacy. A line that measures positive for ketones shows that you have entered a ketosis condition. Most people associate increased ketones level in the body, with a diabetic medical real crisis known as ketoacidosis. Still, there are somewhat distinct conditions, dietary ketosis involved with the keto diet and diabetic ketoacidosis.

1.1 Types of Keto Diet

These are different types of keto diets, available:

• **Standard keto diet:** The diet (SKD) is very small in oil, mild in protein, and extra fat can be utilized. Usually, it comprises 20% protein, 75% fat and just 5 percent carbohydrates.

• **Targeted keto diet:** The plan (TKD) of this diet allows carbohydrates to incorporate into workouts.

• **Cyclical keto diet:** Cyclical keto diet (CKD): involves higher-carbohydrate refeed cycles such as five keto days and then two days of high-carb.

• **High in protein keto diet:** Close to a traditional keto diet, except with extra protein. The composition is often 35% protein, 60% fat, and 5% carbohydrates.

However, scientists have conducted an extensive study of standard and high protein keto diets only. This knowledge often applies to the standard keto diet (SKD); however, many of the same instructions still apply to the other variations. Keto diet is also an important means of losing weight and does not have any disease risk factors. However, studies show that the keto diet is now far beneficial for the people than to the often-prescribed low in the fat diet plan.

The food is also so rich in nutrients; you would lose weight without calorie counting or tracking your dietary intake. One study found that people on a keto diet lost 2.1 significantly more likely than those on a low fat, calorie-limited diet and improved triglyceride and HDL cholesterol rates. Another study has found that people on the keto diet lose three relatively faster than they lose those on a diabetes UK diet. There are other reasons why a keto diet is superior to a low in the fat diet, which includes high protein intake, and has many benefits. The cause may be the reduced ketones, lower cholesterol levels, and enhanced response to insulin. A Keto diet can help you lose weight. Initially, in the first three to six months compared with certain other diets. It could be because more calories are required to transform fat into energy than to convert carbohydrates into energy. A high protein and high-fat diet are more likely to suit you more; maybe you are eating fewer, so it is not yet verified.

Keto Diet with Diabetes and Prediabetes

Diabetes is marked by shifts in appetite, increased blood pressure, and decreased regulation of insulin. The keto diet can help lose excess weight, which is closely correlated with type two diabetes, prediabetes which metabolic syndrome.

Another study carried out by people with type 2 diabetes has found that 7 out of 21 participants could stop using any diabetes medications. On yet another study, the party that followed the keto diet lost 24.4 pounds (11.1 kg) in comparison to 15.2 pounds (6.9 kg) in the higher-carb band. It is a significant benefit when considering the weight-to-type two diabetes connection. By contrast, 95.2 percent of the keto community was also willing to avoid or decrease diabetes treatment, compared to 62 percent of the higher-carb community. Individuals are most inclined to try a keto diet to lose weight, and this may help cure some medical conditions, such as epilepsy. If you practice the keto diet, it can even benefit patients with heart failure, other brain conditions, and wrinkles, although further work has to be done in certain fields. First, you should talk to your doctor about whether it is okay for a person like you to go on a keto diet if you have type 1 diabetes. For starters, a keto diet may help increase strength athletes and runners and cyclists. It increases the muscle to fat ratio over time, increasing the volume of oxygen that the body can absorb when working hard. Thus, it may help in the preparation, high efficiency.

How Does It Work?

The keto diet's purpose is to use a different type of fuel in your body. Rather than focusing on carbohydrate sugar (glucose: such as rice, legumes, beans, and fruits), the keto diet is influenced by ketone bodies, a form of fuel the liver creates from fat. Burning food is an effective way to lose weight. However, making ketone bodies into the liver is tricky:

• You must deprive yourself of carbohydrates, must take less than 50g of carbs each day (remember a small banana contains about more than 25g of carbs).

• It typically takes several days to get to a ketosis state.

• Having too much protein will hinder to get into a ketosis stage.

1.2 Keto Kitchen

What Should You Eat?

Since there is such a great fat element of the keto diet, participants will consume fat in every meal. It would be like 40g of sugars, 165g of weight, and 75g of protein in a regular 2000 calorie (food) diet. Although, the specific amount of nutrients depends on the individual requirements. The keto diet makes certain good unsaturated fats like walnuts, almonds, peas, olive oil, avocados, tofu. Yet largely saturated fats are recommended from oils like palm oil, coconut oil, lard, milk.

Meat is portion of the keto diet but it does not typically distinguish between lean protein products and high source of protein in fat like bacon and pork. Most fruits are high in carbohydrates, but you can get other fruits like blueberries in limited amounts. Vegetables (also high in carbohydrates) are restricted to greens vegetables like black bell peppers, brussels sprouts, kale, spinach, cauliflower, asparagus, mushrooms, onions, celery, garlic, cucumber, and squashes. Even a bowl of broccoli is diced and contains approximately six carbohydrates.

How Can You Follow A Keto Diet?

There are many forms of a keto diet, but you have to drastically decrease the number of carbohydrates you consume to reach a ketosis condition. (The keto tracker can be used to create a custom food plan.) Estimates suggest that the average adult man over the age of 20 absorbs 47.4 %of his daily calories from carbs. The average adult woman over the age of 20 consumes 49.6 % of her daily calories from carbs. Yet 80 to 90 % of calories come from fat, 5 to 15 % come from protein, and 5 to 10 % come from carbs in the standard keto diet, which was first intended to treat seizure disorders. The most widely practiced variation of the plan currently is a simplified form of the keto diet that encourages you to consume protein more liberally — about 20 to 30 %of the daily calories — for the remaining starch limit. Many of a keto diet's new edition goals are weight reduction, weight control, and better athletic results.

The keto diet has been changed variously. Following a keto diet, most individuals follow the so-called traditional keto diet program, which contains approximately 10 % of the overall carbohydrate calories. Other types of keto diets include cyclic keto diets, carb cycling, and guided keto diets that require carbohydrate intake to be changed through exercise. Usually, these changes are introduced by athletes looking to use the keto diet to enhance performance and endurance rather than by focusing on weight loss. Yet broadly speaking, if you intend on adopting a keto diet, you will target eating fewer than 10 % of the total carbohydrate calories a day. The remaining calories should be 20 to 30% calcium and 60 to 80% fat. A recent study suggests that if you eat a 2,000-calorie diet regularly, no more than 200 calories (or 50 g) will come from sugars, whereas 400 to 600 calories will come from protein, and 1,200 to 1,600 from fat. (There is a reason this program is often dubbed a low-carbohydrate, high-fat diet).

Main Ingredients to Be Used in A Keto Diet

How does the keto-friendly shopping bag look like to you?
Clear all enticing carb-heavy products in your pantry and fridge. Snacks with sugar, processed foods, bread and rice, starchy vegetables,
Sweeteners like jellies, honey, jams, agave nectar, and others before you start shopping. The ingredients to make up the pantry basket to make keto recipes for a keto beginner are mentioned below. We propose that you double the

ingredients and proteins to cook together with our recipes at home!

A Regular Keto Diet Catalog of Acceptable Foods:

Proteins

Ingredients
- Breakfast sausage
- Boneless, skinless chicken breasts
- Bacon
- Ground beef

Produce

Ingredients
- White onion
- mushrooms
- Garlic
- Spinach
- Avocado
- Romaine or leaf lettuce
- Green cabbage
- Green onions
- Red bell black pepper
- Cherry tomatoes
- Lime

Eggs and Dairy

Ingredients
- Sea salted butter
- Plain, whole milk yogurt
- Cream cheese
- Eggs
- Blue cheese

Pantry Supplies

Ingredients
- Cocoa powder
- Chicken broth
- Coconut cream
- Monk fruit extract
- Vanilla extract
- Almond flour
- Soy sauce
- Almond butter

Oils and Spices

Ingredients
- Sea salt
- Garlic powder
- Black pepper
- Ground ginger
- Cinnamon
- Coconut oil
- Sesame seed
- Sesame oil
- Avocado oil
- Vegetables with no starch like broccoli, black peppers, mushrooms, onions, leafy greens and cauliflower, cabbage.
- Dairy, including cheese, eggs
- Protein (source) as in soybeans, fish, beef, pork, shellfish, and poultry
- Sunflower seeds, walnuts, peanuts, pistachios, and pumpkin seeds
- Fats, such as cooking oil, butter.

Foods You Should Stop During the Ketogenic Diet or Reduce It

• Processed products such as crackers, chips of maize and packet chips
• Cookies include cookies, cakes, and brownies
• All sorts of grains, including quinoa, bread, rice, and pasta.
• Fruits are rich in carbon like tropical fruits, melons.
• Sweeteners that include Equal, Splenda.
• While both nuts and seeds are low in net carbohydrates, the sum between the various forms differs quite a bit.

Here Are the Carb Counts of Some Common Nuts and Seeds For 2 tbsp.:

• Almonds: 3 grams of carbs net (6 grams of carbs total)
• Brazilian nuts: 1-gram of carbs net (3 grams of carbs total)
• Cashews: 8 grams of carbs net (9 grams of carbs total)
• Macadamia nuts: 2 grams of carbs net (4 grams of carbs total)
• Total pecan: 1 gram of carbs net (4 grams of carbs total)
• Pistachios: 5 grams of carbs net (8 grams of carbs total)
• Walnuts: 2 grams of carbs net (4 grams of carbs total)
• Chia seeds: 1-gram of carbs net (12 grams of carbs total)
• Flaxseeds: 0 grams of carbs net (8 grams of carbs total)
• Pumpkin seeds: 4 grams of carbs net (5 grams of carbs total)
• Sesame seeds 3 grams of carbs net (7 grams of carbs total)

Here are the carb counts of certain berries for 7 tbsp. (100 grams)

• Blackberries: 5 grams of carbs net (10 grams of carbs total)
• Blueberries: 14 grams of carbs net (12 grams of carbs total)
• Raspberries: 6 grams of carbs net (12 grams of carbs total)
• Strawberries: 6 grams of carbs net (8 grams of carbs total)

1.3 Tools to Get Started with Keto

If you are new on a keto diet or an experienced expert-you are already investing some personal time in your kitchen. Given that the keto diet has been increasingly popular lately, there are still not many readily available health products, and we all know the best is homemade. This can be daunting and disappointing for newbies if you are not used to preparing most meals at home. A collection of kitchen equipment and devices are some of the items that only relieve the extra kitchen time.

- Chef's Knife
- Air Fryer
- Egg Slicer
- Silicon Baking Map
- The Instant Pot
- Whoopee, Pie Pan
- Cast Iron Skillet
- Electric Milk Frother
- Silicone Muffin Liners
- Blender and Food Processor
- Vegetable Spiralizer
- Digital Food Scale
- Burger Press
- George Forman Grill
- Instant Pot
- Butter Bell
- Sous Vide Precision Cooker
- Mason Jars
- Food Vacuum Sealer
- Small Hanging Trash Bag
- Instant Read Thermometer

Chapter 2: Foods for Keto Eating

Like any other specific eating plan, the keto diet comes with a list of allowed and foods that aren't allowed. The best way to think of this plan is to focus on all of the delicious foods you can eat and don't worry too much about the things you are leaving behind. You will be eliminating sugary foods and processed foods, leaving your menu options open for meat, low-carb veggies, and the healthy fats that will keep you feeling full and satisfied.

Carbohydrates

The keto diet is a low-carb diet, and eliminating your dependence on carbs causes your body to burn fat for fuel. Some veggies and fruits are allowed on the keto diet, which might seem confusing when the diet is supposed to be low-carb. Your body needs some foods that provide fiber, but the fiber is a carb. The difference is that fiber does not count toward your carb intake because it passes through your body as waste since your body can't digest fiber. So the carb count on the keto diet is always expressed as net carbs, which are the carbs left over when the grams of fiber is subtracted from the total carbohydrate count.

Look for fruits and veggies that are lower in net carbs. You can consume more of these to help you feel full since they are lower in carbs. When it comes to fruits, very few are allowed since most fruits are loaded with fruit sugar, making them higher on the carb count. There are several delicious fruits you can consume on the keto diet. The following lists allowed fruits and their carb count for a half-cup serving:

FRUIT	NET CARBS
Raspberries	4
Strawberries	5
Blackberries	4
Blueberries	4
Watermelon	6
Cantaloupe	6
Lemon	1
Lime	1
Rhubarb	2
Star Fruit	3

More veggies are allowed on the keto diet than fruits, and these will help round out your menu options. The best veggies to consume on the keto diet are the ones listed below. The carb count shown is for a one-cup serving.

VEGETABLE	NET CARBS
Artichokes	4
Cabbage, red/green	2
Eggplant	6
Onions	5
Radishes	2
Tomatoes	4
Celery	1
Brussel sprouts	4
Cucumbers	3
Kale	6
Garlic, one clove	1
Lettuce, all types	1
Green beans	6
Cauliflower	2
Avocados	3

Spinach	1
Zucchini	3
Mushrooms	1
Asparagus	4
Broccoli	4
Bell peppers, all colors	5

Most meats, fish, and seafood are carb-free, but there are some exceptions. Seafood that comes in a shell, like lobster, clams, scallops, and oyster, do have some carbs. Like deli meat and prepared meat like hot dogs, some meats may have a low carb count. The best way to avoid carbs here is to eat meats that are whole meats and not prepared, although the ready varieties can be used. Check the label for the carb count and go with the lowest one possible. The meats you consume will be one of your best sources of fat on the keto diet. The rest of your fats will come from heart-healthy oils, cheese, yogurt, and eggs. When you purchase dairy items, always get the full-fat variety.

You should stock some added items in your kitchen since they will fill out your meal plans and be used as a quick snack when hunger threatens to derail your efforts. These foods include the following:

Canned tuna	Coffee	Club soda
Pork rinds	Olives	Pickles
Mustard	Broth	Sugar-free flavored water

When you shop for groceries, plan your menus first, and buy only the foods you need to complete your meal plans. This process will help you avoid purchasing those items you do not need to eat. Only purchase the foods you know you will eat, since it makes no sense to buy something because it is allowed if you don't like the taste. This plan is a lifestyle change, so you need to live with the food choices you make. Do not be afraid to try foods you might not have liked before because your tastes change as you get older. While fresh foods are preferred, you might not eat all of your fresh produce before it spoils, so frozen is also acceptable.

While processed meats can help fill out your meal plans occasionally, do not rely on processed foods more than you need to. The keto diet is based on real, fresh food that you prepare yourself. This process will take planning, but you will succeed, and soon it will be second nature. You will not be deprived of good tasting food, and you will still enjoy the occasional dessert. Achievement with the keto diet requires planning and creativity, and you might be pleasantly surprised at how flexible this plan is.

Chapter 3: Fourteen Day Meal Plan

All of the recipes featured in this meal plan are found in this recipe book. Feel free to mix the suggestions to suit your needs.

WEEK ONE

DAY ONE
Breakfast: Dairy-Free Cinnamon Latte
Lunch: Chicken Soup
Dinner: Easy Mongolian Beef

DAY TWO
Breakfast: Coconut Porridge
Lunch: Quesadillas
Dinner: Pesto Chicken Casserole

DAY THREE
Breakfast: Oven Bacon Omelet
Lunch: Shrimp with Artichokes
Dinner: Pork Stir Fry

DAY FOUR
Breakfast: Seafood Omelet
Lunch: Bacon Burger Casserole
Dinner: Creamy Spinach Feta Chicken

DAY FIVE
Breakfast: Pumpkin Spice Egg Loaf
Lunch: Deviled Egg Salad
Dinner: Garlic Pork Tenderloin

DAY SIX
Breakfast: Blueberry Pancakes Bites
Lunch: Sausage Stuffed Mushrooms
Dinner: Lemon Dill Tuna Cakes

DAY SEVEN
Breakfast: Strawberry Smoothie
Lunch: Italian Style Keto Plate
Dinner: Garlic Butter Salmon

WEEK TWO

DAY ONE
Breakfast: Cinnamon Roll Coffee Cake
Lunch: Caesar Salad
Dinner: Spaghetti Squash Cheeseburger Casserole

DAY TWO
Breakfast: Avocado and Boiled Eggs
Lunch: Spicy Chicken Casserole
Dinner: Shrimp and Sausage Skillet

DAY THREE
Breakfast: Eggplant Benedict
Lunch: Hamburger Gratin with Brussels sprouts
Dinner: Caprese Chicken

DAY FOUR
Breakfast: Brussels sprouts and Eggs
Lunch: Club Salad
Dinner: Spanish Style Cauliflower Rice

DAY FIVE
Breakfast: Fried Eggs with Pork and Spinach
Lunch: Avocado Cheese Salad
Dinner: Brussel sprouts and Asian Shrimp

DAY SIX
Breakfast: Curried Eggs
Lunch: Cauliflower Soup
Dinner: Sausage Alfredo

DAY SEVEN
Breakfast: Ranch Style Scrambled Eggs
Lunch: Curried Whitefish with Broccoli
Dinner: Cheesy Cabbage and Smoked Sausage

Chapter 4: Breakfast Recipes

You can fry some eggs and place them besides ham or bacon with a slice of tomato for a perfect keto breakfast, but there are times when you might want something a bit more exciting for breakfast. These recipes will please the fussiest eaters.

Oven Bacon Omelet
Nutrition facts: Calories 737/Protein 21g/Carbs 2g/Fat 72g/Fiber 3g

Total Prep & Cook Time: 25 minutes

Yields: 2 servings

Estimated cost: $8.10

Ingredients:

- Butter, 3 ounces
- Black pepper, ½ teaspoon
- Fresh chives, chopped finely, 1 tablespoon
- Eggs, 4
- Fresh bacon, 6 slices cut into chunks
- Chopped fresh spinach, ¼ cup
- Salt, ½ teaspoon
- Rosemary, ½ teaspoon

Method:

1. Warm your oven to 400 F.
2. Use half the butter to coat an eight-inch baking dish.

3. Fry the spinach and bacon chunks together in the other half of the butter.
4. While they are frying, beat the eggs well.
5. Put the fried spinach and bacon into the beaten eggs.
6. Mix in the seasonings.
7. Put the ingredients into the baking pan and cover with chopped chives.
8. Bake the dish for 20 minutes.

Dairy-Free Cinnamon Latte

Nutrition facts: Calories 191/Protein 6g/Carbs 1g/Fat 18g/Fiber 1g

Total Prep & Cook Time: 5 minutes

Yields: 2 servings

Estimated cost: $4.00

Ingredients:

- Vanilla extract, 2 teaspoons
- Eggs, 2
- Ginger, ground, 1 teaspoon
- Coconut oil, 3 tablespoons
- Ground cinnamon, 2 teaspoons
- Boiling water, 1 ½ cups

Method:

1. Except for the eggs, add all of the ingredients in a blender.
2. Break the eggs into a bowl.
3. Pour the eggs into the blender and blend the ingredients immediately, so the eggs do not cook.
4. Serve immediately.

Ranch-Style Scrambled Eggs

Nutrition facts: Calories 229/Protein 14g/Carbs 2g/Fat 18g/Fiber 7g

Total Prep & Cook Time: 25 minutes

Yields: 4 servings

Estimated cost: $7.65

Ingredients:

- Diced bell pepper, any color, ½ cup
- Chili powder, ¼ teaspoon
- Eggs, 6
- Diced tomato, ½ cup
- Black pepper, ½ teaspoon
- Scallion, 1 finely chopped
- Salt, ½ teaspoon
- Shredded cheddar cheese, ½ cup
- Jalapeno pepper, 1 minced
- Butter, 3 tablespoons

Method:

1. Fry the tomatoes, bell pepper, jalapeno, and scallions in the melted butter for 5 minutes.
2. Beat the eggs with the seasonings.
3. Pour the beaten eggs over the veggies in the skillet.
4. Stir the eggs well until they are scrambled to your preference.
5. Add in the cheese and cook, stirring well, for two minutes.

Avocado and Boiled Eggs

Nutrition facts: Calories 316/Protein 11g/Carbs 1g/Fat 29g/Fiber 4g

Total Prep & Cook Time: 20 minutes

Yields: 4 servings

Ingredients:

- Avocado, 2
- Mayonnaise, 8 tablespoons
- Ground paprika, 1 tablespoon
- Chopped parsley, 1 tablespoon
- Eggs, 8

Method:

1. Boil the eggs for 10 minutes undisturbed.
2. Dump the water off and peel the boiled eggs, then slice thinly.
3. Set out two serving plates and divide the egg slices evenly between them.
4. Peel, pit, and slice the avocado and divide the slices evenly between the two plates.
5. Blend the parsley and paprika into the mayonnaise, and place a dollop of mayonnaise on each plate.

Strawberry Smoothie

Nutrition facts: Calories 415/Protein 6g/Carbs 8g/Fat 43g/Fiber 8g

Total Prep & Cook Time: 10 minutes

Yields: 2 servings

Estimated cost: $5.25

Ingredients:

Coconut milk, 2 cups

Vanilla extract, 1 tablespoon

Cinnamon, 1 tablespoon

Fresh or frozen strawberries, ½ cup sliced

Lime or lemon juice, 2 tablespoons

Method:

1. Place in your blender the coconut milk, lemon juice, vanilla, and strawberries and blend well.
2. Pour the smoothie into two serving glasses.
3. Top with the ground cinnamon and enjoy.

Coconut Porridge

Nutrition facts: Calories 481/Protein 9g/Carbs 4g/Fat 48g/Fiber 9g

Total Prep & Cook Time: 15 minutes

Yields: 1 serving

Estimated cost: $5.25

Ingredients:

- Egg, 1
- Coconut cream, 4 tablespoons
- Ground cinnamon, 1 teaspoon
- Coconut Flour, 1 tablespoon
- Ground nutmeg, ½ teaspoon
- Coconut oil, 1 tablespoon
- Ground psyllium husk powder, ¼ teaspoon
- Salt, ½ teaspoon

Method:

1. Blend the coconut flour, salt, cinnamon, nutmeg, egg, and psyllium husk powder.
2. Stir the coconut oil and coconut cream together in a small pot.
3. Slowly stir in the egg mixture, stirring continuously.
4. Cook this over medium heat until it is creamy and slightly thick.
5. Put the mixture into a serving bowl and drop on a handful of raspberries or blueberries if desired.

Brussel Sprouts and Eggs

Nutrition facts: Calories 347/Protein 20g/Carbs 11g/Fat 16g/Fiber 7g

Total Prep & Cook Time: 25 minutes

Yields: 2 servings

Estimated cost: $6.25

Ingredients:

- Olive oil, 3 tablespoons
- Black pepper, 1 teaspoon
- Freshly grated Brussel sprouts, 2 cups
- Eggs, 2
- Rosemary, ½ teaspoon
- Salt, ½ teaspoon

Method:

1. Fry the shredded Brussel sprouts in olive oil for 8 to 10 minutes, often stirring, until they begin to turn brown.
2. Spread the cooked sprouts to the side with a spoon to create two hollows in the mixture.
3. Break one of the eggs into each of the hollow places.
4. Let the eggs fry for 5 minutes, not disturbing the mixture.
5. Sprinkle the top with the rosemary, salt, and pepper and serve.

Curried Eggs

Nutrition facts: Calories 186/Protein 7g/Carbs 3g/Fat 13g/Fiber 2g

Total Prep & Cook Time: 20 minutes

Yields: 2 servings

Estimated cost: $6.75

Ingredients:

- Eggs, 6
- Cumin, ground, 1 teaspoon
- Salt, 1 teaspoon
- Paprika, 1 teaspoon
- Diced onion, ½ cup
- Turmeric, ground, ½ teaspoon
- Diced tomato, ½ cup
- Minced garlic, 3 tablespoons
- Water, ½ cup
- Chili powder, ½ teaspoon
- Powdered coriander, 2 teaspoons

Method:

1. Fry the garlic and onion in butter for five minutes.
2. Put in the spices and tomatoes and cook for three more minutes.
3. Pour in the water and cook for three more minutes.
4. Beat the eggs well.
5. Pour the beaten eggs over the mixture in the skillet, blend well, and then stir until the eggs are scrambled.

Seafood Omelet

Nutrition facts: Calories 672/Protein 27g/Carbs 4g/Fat 63g/Fiber 5g

Total Prep & Cook Time: 20 minutes

Yield: 2 servings

Estimated cost: $9.55

Ingredients:

- Shredded Swiss cheese, ½ cup
- Cooked small Shrimp, ½ cup
- Red pepper flakes, ½ teaspoon
- Minced garlic, 2 tablespoons
- Dried thyme, ¼ teaspoon
- Olive oil, 2 tablespoons
- Mayonnaise, ½ cup
- Butter, 3 tablespoons
- Salt, ½ teaspoons
- Black pepper, 1 teaspoon
- Eggs, 6
- Freshly chopped chives, 3 tablespoons
- Ground cumin, ½ teaspoon
- Freshly chopped parsley, 2 tablespoons

Method:

1. Cover the shrimp with oil.
2. Fry the chives with the garlic in hot olive oil for three minutes.
3. Beat the eggs with the pepper flakes, cumin, pepper, thyme, and salt.
4. Fry the eggs for five minutes undisturbed.

5. Put in the Shrimp and the shredded cheese to the omelet and fold it in half in the skillet.
6. Cook the omelet for three more minutes on each side.
7. Dribble with chopped parsley and serve with the mayonnaise on the side.

Fried Eggs with Pork and Spinach

Nutrition facts: Calories 382/Protein 24g/Carbs 8g/Fat 32g/Fiber 4g

Total Prep & Cook Time: 40 minute

Yields: 2 servings

Estimated cost: $8.75

Ingredients:

- Smoked pork loin, 8 ounces cut into bite-sized chunks
- Eggs, 4
- Frozen cranberries, thawed, ¼ cup
- Butter, 3 tablespoons
- Salt, ½ teaspoon
- Black pepper, 1 teaspoon
- Baby spinach, chopped, 2 cups
- Walnuts, chopped, ¼ cup

Method:

1. Fry the chopped spinach in the butter for 5 minutes, stirring often.
2. Scoop out the cooked spinach and drain.
3. Put the pork loin in the skillet and fry for 5 minutes.
4. Stir the cranberries and walnuts into the skillet with the spinach and fry for five more minutes, stirring often.
5. Scoop out this mixture and place it in a serving bowl.
6. Fry the eggs in the skillet to your preferred doneness.
7. Put two fried eggs on each plate and divide the pork between the serving plates.

Pumpkin Spice Egg Loaf

Nutrition facts: Calories 277/Protein 8g/Carbs 3g/Fat 23g/Fiber 1g

Total Prep & Cook Time: 33 minutes

Yields: 2 servings

Estimated cost: $2.75

Ingredients:

- Butter, softened, 2 tablespoons
- Cream cheese, softened, 2 ounces
- Pureed pumpkin, 2 tablespoons
- Pumpkin pie spice, 1 teaspoon
- Eggs, 2
- Stevia, 1 tablespoon

Method:

1. Warm your oven to 350 F.
2. Grease two eight-ounce oven-safe bowls.
3. Blend everything in your blender until they are creamy.
4. Bake for twenty-five minutes.
5. The mixture will puff while it cooks and sinks a bit when removed from the oven.
6. Sprinkle cinnamon on top to serve.

Eggplant Benedict

Nutrition facts: Calories 634/Protein 28g/Carbs 5g/Fat 54g/Fiber 2g

Total Prep & Cook Time: 45 minutes

Yields: 2 servings

Estimated cost: $6.95

Ingredients:

- Egg yolks, 2
- Olive oil, 2 tablespoons
- Salt, ¼ teaspoon
- Paprika for garnish
- Lemon juice, 2 teaspoons
- Eggplant slices, 4, 1/2-inch thick
- Black pepper, ½ teaspoon
- Ham or bacon, 4 slices cooked crisply
- Melted butter, ¼ cup
- Cayenne pepper, 1/8 teaspoon
- Eggs, 4
- Vinegar, 2 tablespoons

Method:

1. Simmer the lemon juice and egg yolks in the top part of a double boiler.
2. Drizzle in the cayenne pepper and melted butter while continuously stirring.
3. When this is thick, set it to the side, covered, while you prepare the rest.
4. Pepper and salt the eggplant slices and fry in the oil for four to five minutes on each side.

5. Poach the eggs in a skillet of boiling water for three minutes.
6. Put two eggplant slices each on two serving plates.
7. Lay one poached egg on each eggplant slice.
8. Stir the sauce and drizzle it over the eggs and sprinkle on paprika to serve.

Blueberry Pancake Bites

Nutrition facts: Calories 188/Protein 6g/Carbs 5g/Fat 14g/Fiber 4g

Total Prep & Cook Time: 45 minutes

Yields: 6 servings (24 bites, 4 per serving)

Estimated cost: $5.80

Ingredients:

- Melted butter, ¼ cup
- Salt, ¼ teaspoon
- Frozen blueberries, ½ cup
- Cinnamon, 1 teaspoon
- Vanilla extract, ½ teaspoon
- Baking powder, 1 teaspoon
- Eggs, 4
- Stevia, ¼ cup
- Coconut flour, ½ cup
- Water, ½ cup

Method:

1. Warm your oven to 350 F.
2. Grease a twenty-four cup mini muffin pan.
3. Mix in your blender the cinnamon, salt, baking powder, melted butter, and coconut flour until smooth.
4. Let the batter sit undisturbed for five minutes, then add the water and blend again.
5. Add the batter equally to the muffin cups.
6. Press four or five blueberries into each muffin.
7. Bake for twenty-five minutes, until done, and then serve hot or cold.

Cinnamon Roll Coffee Cake

Nutrition facts: Calories 223/Protein 7g/Carbs 4g/Fat 19g/Fiber 3g

Total Prep & Cook Time: 50 minutes

Yields: 16 servings

Estimated cost: $7.25

Ingredients:

- FOR THE CAKE
    - Melted butter, ½ cup
    - Almond milk, ½ cup
    - Vanilla extract, 1 teaspoon
    - Eggs, 3
    - Salt, ½ teaspoon
    - Baking powder, 2 teaspoon
    - Whey protein powder, unflavored, ¼ cup
    - Stevia, ¾ cup
    - Almond Flour, 3 cups

- FOR THE FILLING
    - Ground cinnamon, 2 teaspoon
    - Stevia, 3 tablespoons

- FOR THE FROSTING
    - Vanilla extract, ½ teaspoon
    - Heavy whipping cream, 1 tablespoon
    - Powdered stevia, 2 tablespoons
    - Softened cream cheese, 3 tablespoons

Method:

1. Warm your oven to 325 F.
2. Oil an eight-inch oven pan.
3. Blend the ingredients for the filling and set off to the side.
4. Mix the salt, baking powder, protein powder, almond flour, and sweetener for the cake batter.
5. Add in the almond milk, melted butter, vanilla extract, and eggs and blend until the batter is smooth.
6. Put half of the batter in the baking dish and smooth.
7. Sprinkle two-thirds of the filling mix on the batter in the baking dish.
8. Pour in the remainder of the cake batter and smooth.
9. Bake for thirty to thirty-five minutes.
10. Sprinkle the leftover cinnamon filling mixture on top of the cake.
11. Cream the ingredients for the frosting and drizzle or pipe it on top of the cake.

Zucchini Spice Waffles

Nutrition facts: Calories 239/Protein 9g/Carbs 5g/Fats 23g/Fiber 6g

Total Prep & Cook Time: 90 minutes

Yields: 8 waffles (servings)

Estimated cost: $7.25

Ingredients:

- Shredded zucchini, 1 ½ cups
- Baking powder, 1 tablespoon
- Egg white, 2
- Cinnamon, 1 ½ teaspoon
- Avocado oil, ¼ cup
- Eggs, 2
- Stevia, ¼ cup
- Vanilla extract, 1 teaspoon
- Salt, ½ teaspoon
- Almond Flour, 2 cups
- Water, ¼ cup
- Ground ginger, ½ teaspoon

Method:

1. Drop the shredded zucchini in a colander in your sink and sprinkle one teaspoon of salt on it. Cover it with paper towels and set a bowl on top, to press the liquid out of the zucchini. Let this sit for one hour.
2. Heat your waffle iron and grease if needed.
3. Stir the ginger, cinnamon, baking powder, stevia, and almond flour until the batter is smooth.

4. Mix in the vanilla extract, water, avocado oil, egg whites, eggs, and the drained zucchini until well mixed.
5. Add about one-fourth cup of batter, and cook the waffles until done.

Chapter 5: Lunch Recipes

Italian Style Keto Plate

Nutrition facts: Calories 722/Protein 40g/Carbs 8g/Fat 69g/Fiber 6g

Total Prep & Cook Time: 15 minutes

Yields: 2 servings

Estimated cost: $7.75

Ingredients:

- Grape tomatoes, ½ cup
- Green olives, 20
- Olive oil, ¼ cup
- Sliced prosciutto or salami, 8 ounces
- Freshly sliced mozzarella cheese, 8 ounces
- Salt and pepper as needed

Method:

1. Set out two serving plates.
2. Equally, divide the items between the two plates.
3. Use salt and pepper as needed.

Quesadillas

Nutrition facts: Calories 473/Protein 21g/Carbs 5g/Fat 41g/Fiber 5g

Total Prep & Cook Time: 30 minutes

Yields: 4 servings

Estimated cost: $7.25

Ingredients:

- Chopped baby spinach, ½ cup
- Eggs, 3
- Shredded Mexican blend cheese, ¾ cup
- Softened cream cheese, 6 ounces
- Olive oil, 2 tablespoons
- Salt, ¼ teaspoon
- Coconut Flour, 1 tablespoon
- Ground psyllium husk powder, 2 teaspoons

Method:

1. Warm your oven to 400 F.
2. Beat the eggs until they are slightly foamy.
3. Beat the cream cheese into the eggs until the batter is creamy.
4. Blend the salt, psyllium husk powder, and coconut flour in another bowl.
5. Stir continuously while pouring the egg mixture into the flour ingredients and stir until creamy.
6. Let this batter sit undisturbed for five minutes.
7. Cover a baking flat with foil or parchment paper.
8. Spread the batter into a rectangle in the baking flat and cook for six to nine minutes, or until slightly brown.

9. Slice this batter into eight smaller pieces.
10. Lay one tortilla in a hot skillet in olive oil.
11. Cover the tortilla with shredded cheese and spinach, and lay another tortilla on top.
12. Cook each quesadilla for two minutes on each side.

Avocado Cheese Salad

Nutrition facts: Calories 751/Protein 27g/Carbs 6g/Fat 73g/Fiber 6g

Total Prep & Cook Time: 30 minutes

Yields: 4 servings

Estimated cost: $7.15

Ingredients:

- Sharp cheddar cheese, cubed, 1 cup
- Avocado, 2 peeled and sliced
- Chopped arugula, ½ cup
- Bacon, 8 slices
- Mayonnaise, ½ cup
- Black pepper, ½ teaspoon
- Salt, ¼ teaspoon
- Heavy whipping cream, 3 tablespoons
- Chopped walnuts, ¼ cup
- Minced garlic, 2 tablespoons
- Minced onions, ¼ cup

Method:

1. Warm your oven to 400 F.
2. Grease a thirteen by nine-inch oven dish.
3. Place the chunks of cheese in the oven dish.
4. Cook the bacon until crispy and crumble it over the cheese.
5. Sprinkle the minced garlic and onions over the bacon.
6. Bake the cheese for 5 minutes until it is softened.
7. Set out four serving plates.
8. Equally, divide the sliced avocado and chopped arugula between the four plates.

9. Divide the cheese bacon mixture between the four plates.
10. Cream together the lemon juice, pepper, salt, mayonnaise, olive oil, and whipping cream and drizzle this over the four plates and serve.

Chicken Soup

Nutrition facts: Calories 509/Protein 33g/Carbs 4g/Fat 40g/Fiber 7g

Total Prep & Cook Time: 40 minutes

Yields: 8 servings

Estimated cost: $6.95

Ingredients:

- Dried rosemary, 1 teaspoon
- Chopped carrots, ¼ cup
- Button mushrooms, 1 small can
- Chopped celery, ¼ cup
- Chunked cooked chicken, 4 cups
- Chicken broth, 8 cups
- Minced onion, 2 tablespoons
- Parsley, chopped fresh, 2 tablespoons
- Black pepper, 1 teaspoon
- Shredded green cabbage, 1 cup
- Salt, 1 teaspoon
- Minced garlic, 3 tablespoons

Method:

1. Fry the garlic, carrot, onion, celery, and mushrooms in the butter in a large pot for five minutes, stirring often.
2. Blend in the broth with rosemary, parsley, salt, and pepper.
3. Let the soup cook for fifteen minutes.
4. Put in the chicken chunks and shredded cabbage, and simmer the soup for ten more minutes to let the cabbage get tender.

Spicy Chicken Casserole

Nutrition facts: Calorie 748/Protein 57g/Carbs 10g/Fat 68g/Fiber 6g

Total Prep & Cook Time: 40 minutes

Yields: 4 servings

Estimated cost: $7.95

Ingredients:

- Red pepper flakes, ½ teaspoon
- Chunked cooked chicken, 2 cups
- Chili powder, ½ teaspoon
- Bell pepper, yellow or red, chopped, ½ cup
- Sharp cheddar cheese, shredded, 1 cup
- Salt, ½ teaspoon
- Chopped yellow onion, ¼ cup
- Mayonnaise, ½ cup
- Cream cheese, 8 ounces soften to room temperature

Method:

1. Warm your oven to 400 F.
2. Blend the chicken chunks into half of the shredded cheese.
3. Put in the mayonnaise, pepper flakes, chili powder, salt, cream cheese, and the onions and peppers.
4. Grease an 8-inch oven dish.
5. Put the chicken in the baking pan and cover with the other half of the cheese.
6. Bake the casserole uncovered for 20 minutes.

Sausage Stuffed Mushrooms

Nutrition facts: Calories 345/Protein 15g/Carbs 4g/Fat 17g/Fiber 5g

Total Prep & Cook Time: 35 minutes

Yields: 4 servings

Estimated cost: $5.75

Ingredients:

- Butter, 3 tablespoons
- Salt, ¼ teaspoons
- Diced yellow onion, ¼ cup
- Shredded sharp cheddar cheese, 1 cup
- Black pepper, ½ teaspoon
- Link sausage, 4 any style
- Minced garlic, 2 tablespoons
- Baby Bella mushrooms, 20

Method:

1. Warm your oven to 345 F.
2. Wash the mushrooms well and pat them dry.
3. Pull off the mushroom stalks and mince them.
4. Mince the sausage links and fry them in butter for seven minutes.
5. Put in the garlic, minced mushroom stalks, and onion and fry for four more minutes.
6. Stir in the pepper, salt, and shredded cheese.
7. Use the mix to fill the caps and bake for 20 minutes.

Caesar Salad

Nutrition facts: Calories 661/Protein 22g/Carbs 5g/Fat 75g/Fiber 8g

Total Prep & Cook Time: 30 minutes

Yields: 2 servings

Estimated cost: $8.85

Ingredients:

- Dried rosemary, 1 tablespoon
- Black pepper, ½ teaspoon
- Chopped anchovies, 1 tablespoon
- Salt, ½ teaspoon
- Grated parmesan cheese, ½ cup
- Minced garlic, 1 tablespoon
- Bacon, 4 slices
- Chunked cooked chicken breast, 1 ½ cup
- Mayonnaise, ½ cup
- Minced onion, ¼ cup
- Dijon mustard, 2 tablespoons
- Chopped Romaine lettuce, 1 cup

Method:

1. Fry the bacon and crumble it, then lay it on a paper towel to drain.
2. Blend the mayonnaise, Dijon mustard, lemon juice, parmesan cheese, garlic, and chopped anchovies until creamy, and chill while you assemble the salad.
3. Set out two serving plates.
4. Divide the lettuce evenly between the two plates.
5. Divide the chicken chunks evenly between the two plates and lay them on the lettuce.

6. Sprinkle on the minced onion and bacon crumbles.
7. Sprinkle on the parmesan cheese and serve the salads with the dressing.

Cauliflower Soup

Nutrition facts: Calories 535/Protein 8g/Carbs 6g/Fat 78g/Fiber 10g

Total Prep & Cook Time: 30 minutes

Yields: 6 servings

Estimated cost: $6.75

Ingredients:

- Cream cheese, 8-ounce block softened
- Minced garlic, 2 tablespoons
- Dijon mustard, 2 tablespoons
- Rosemary, 1 teaspoon
- Chicken broth, 4 cups
- Cauliflower florets, 2 cups
- Paprika, 1 teaspoon
- Bacon, 6 slices
- Dried parsley, 1 tablespoon
- Salt, ½ teaspoon
- Chopped pecans, ¼ cup
- Black pepper, 1 teaspoon
- Butter, 4 tablespoons

Method:

1. Fry the bacon in the butter for 5 to 8 minutes or until crisp, crumbling as you cook it.
2. Put in the pecans, garlic, and paprika and fry for three more minutes.
3. Pour this into a large deep pot.
4. Stir in the cauliflower, broth, salt, pepper, and rosemary.
5. Boil the soup, and then simmer for fifteen minutes.

6. Put in the mustard and the cream cheese.
7. Puree the soup and then cook for five more minutes to ensure the soup is warm enough.

Shrimp with Artichokes

Nutrition facts: Calories 630/Protein 36g/Carbs 7g/Fat 61g/Fiber 6g

Total Prep & Cook Time: 25 minutes

Yields: 2 servings

Estimated cost: $7.95

Ingredients:

- Canned artichokes, 1 14- to 15-ounce can
- Chopped baby spinach, 2 cups
- Mayonnaise, ½ cup
- Tomato, 1 large
- Olive oil, 4 tablespoons
- Cooked Shrimp, 1 ½ cups peeled and deveined
- Hardboiled eggs, chilled, 4
- Salt and pepper as needed

Method:

1. Set out two plates for serving.
2. Thinly slice the peeled eggs and divide the slices between the two plates.
3. Evenly divide the chilled Shrimp between the two plates.
4. Divide the sliced tomato between the plates.
5. Add the artichoke to the serving plates.
6. Place one dollop of mayonnaise on each plate.
7. Dribble each serving with oil and use pepper and salt as desired.

Hamburger Gratin with Brussel Sprouts

Nutrition facts: Calories 670/Protein 42g/Carbs 8g/Fat 62g/Fiber 7g

Total Prep & Cook Time: 40 minutes

Yields: 4 servings

Estimated cost: $9.50

Ingredients:

- Salt, ½ teaspoon
- Butter, 3 tablespoons
- Ground beef, 1 pound
- Sour cream, 4 tablespoons
- Black pepper, ½ teaspoon
- Brussel sprouts, 1 pound sliced in halves
- Dried thyme, ¼ teaspoon
- Bacon, 8 slices
- Italian seasoning, 1 tablespoon
- Shredded sharp cheddar cheese, 1 cup

Method:

1. Warm your oven to 425 F.
2. Cook the Brussel sprouts and bacon in the butter for 5 minutes.
3. Grease an 8-inch baking dish.
4. Put in the sour cream with the cooked bacon and Brussel sprouts until blended.
5. Pour this into the baking pan.
6. Fry the ground beef for eight to ten minutes, often stirring to crumble as it cooks.
7. Stir the pepper, thyme, salt, and Italian seasoning into the beef.

8. Pour the beef into the baking pan and coat it with shredded cheese.
9. Cook the casserole for 20 minutes.

Deviled Egg Salad

Nutrition facts: Calories 245/Protein 13g/Carbs 2g/Fat 20g/Fiber 3g

Total Prep & Cook Time: 20 minutes

Yields: 6 servings

Estimated cost: $4.85

Ingredients:

- Paprika, ½ teaspoon
- Salt, ½ teaspoon
- Diced celery, 1 stalk
- Apple cider vinegar, 1 tablespoon
- Sliced green onion, 2
- Dijon mustard, 2 tablespoons
- Black pepper, 1 teaspoon
- Mayonnaise, 6 tablespoons
- Hardboiled eggs, 12 chilled

Method:

1. Cut the peeled eggs into bite-sized chunks.
2. Blend the mayonnaise, paprika, vinegar, pepper, salt, and mustard until smooth.
3. Put in the red pepper flakes if desired.
4. Stir in the celery, onion, and egg to the mayonnaise music.
5. Serve the salad with leafy greens if desired.

Club Salad

Nutrition facts: Calories 330/Protein 17g/Carbs 5g/Fat 27g/Fiber 8g

Total Prep & Cook Time: 20 minutes

Yields: 4 servings

Estimated cost: $6.95

Ingredients:

- Chopped Romaine lettuce, 3 cups
- Cubed Swiss cheese, 1 cup
- Onion powder, ½ teaspoon
- Diced cucumber, 1 cup
- Dijon mustard, 1 tablespoon
- Garlic powder, ½ teaspoon
- Sour cream, 2 tablespoons
- Hardboiled eggs, 4 sliced
- Dried parsley, 1 teaspoon
- Mayonnaise, 2 tablespoons

Method:

1. Blend the herbs with the mayonnaise and sour cream.
2. Divide the chopped lettuce into four serving bowls.
3. Divide the veggies, sliced eggs, and cheese cubes into the four bowls.
4. Put a dollop of Dijon mustard in the middle of each salad.
5. Serve the salads with the premixed sour cream dressing.

Bacon Burger Casserole

Nutrition facts: Calories 841/Protein 47g/Carbs 8g/Fat 71g/Fiber 6g

Total Prep & Cook Time: 40 minutes

Yields: 4 servings

Estimated cost: $9.50

Ingredients:

- Shredded cheddar cheese, 1 cup
- Sliced bacon, 8
- Salt, 1 teaspoon
- Butter, 1 tablespoon
- Heavy whipping cream, 1 cup
- Black pepper, 1 teaspoon
- Chopped dill pickles, 2
- Diced tomatoes, 1 cup
- Minced garlic, 2 tablespoons
- Ground beef, 1 pound
- Tomato paste, 2 tablespoons
- Eggs, 2

Method:

1. Heat your oven to 400 F.
2. Fry the bacon in butter for five minutes.
3. Put the beef in the skillet and fry for ten minutes, crumbling the meat as you stir.
4. Mix in the diced pickle, garlic, tomatoes, seasonings, and two-thirds of the shredded cheese.
5. Grease an eight-inch baking dish.
6. Stir the heavy cream, eggs, and tomato paste together and add this to the meat mixture.

7. Put the meat into the baking pan and cover it with the leftover shredded cheese.
8. Bake the casserole for twenty minutes.

Curried Whitefish with Broccoli

Nutrition facts: Calories 785/Protein 42g/Carbs 9g/Fat 65g/Fiber 9g

Total Prep & Cook Time: 35 minutes

Yields: 4 servings

Estimated cost: $9.45

Ingredients:

- Butter, 4 tablespoons
- Red or green curry paste, 2 tablespoons
- Coconut cream, 14 ounces
- Freshly chopped cilantro, ½ cup
- Broccoli florets, 2 cups
- Black pepper, 1 teaspoon
- Salt, ½ teaspoon
- Whitefish, 4 pieces 6 ounces each

Method:

1. Warm the oven to 400 F.
2. Oil a rectangular oven dish.
3. Pepper and salt the fish pieces, put them in the baking dish, and then top each piece with a slice of butter.
4. Cream the curry paste, chopped cilantro, and coconut cream and spoon this mixture over the fish.
5. Bake the fish for twenty minutes.
6. Boil the broccoli for five minutes while the fish is cooking.

Chapter 6: Dinner Recipes

Spaghetti Squash Cheeseburger Casserole

Nutrition facts: Calories 431/Protein 31g/Carbs 7g/Fat 29g/Fiber 2g

Total Prep & Cook Time: 90 minutes

Yields: 6 servings

Estimated cost: $9.75

Ingredients:

- Shredded sharp cheddar cheese, 1 ½ cups
- Ground beef, 1 pound
- Worcestershire sauce, 2 teaspoons
- Salt, ½ teaspoon
- Minced garlic, 2 tablespoons
- Sliced bacon, 4 chopped
- Sugar-free ketchup, 2 tablespoons
- Spaghetti squash, 1 medium-sized
- Black pepper, ½ teaspoon

Method:

1. Heat your oven to 400.
2. Grease a baking pan.
3. Cut open the squash in half from end to end and pull out the seeds.
4. Bake the squash cut side down for 40 minutes.
5. Fry the bacon chunks until they are crisp, then drain on a paper towel.
6. Fry the meat in the leftover bacon fat.

7. Put in the pepper, garlic, and salt, and cook for three more minutes.
8. Mix in the Worcestershire and ketchup.
9. Scoop out the baked squash and mix it with the beef mixture.
10. Cover the meat with the shredded cheese and let the cheese melt, about 5 minutes.

Pesto Chicken Casserole

Nutrition facts: Calories 807/Protein 38g/Carbs 6g/Fat 81g/Fiber 3g

Total Prep & Cook Time: 45 minutes

Yields: 4 servings

Estimated cost: $7.85

Ingredients:

- Minced garlic, 1 tablespoon
- Diced feta cheese, ¾ cup
- Red or green pesto, 1/3 cup
- Coconut oil, 2 tablespoons
- Pepper and salt as need
- Heavy whipping cream, 1 ¼ cup
- Boneless chicken thighs, 2 pounds
- Pitted black olives, 2/3 cup
- Leafy greens any style, 2 cups

Method:

1. Warm your oven to 425 F.
2. Chop the thighs and season them.
3. Fry the thighs in the coconut oil for 10 minutes, often stirring while the chicken browns.
4. Blend the pesto into the whipping cream.
5. Grease a nine-inch baking dish.
6. Put the chicken into the baking pan with the pesto, garlic, cheese, and olives.
7. Bake this for 25 minutes.

Easy Mongolian Beef

Nutrition facts: Calories 417/Protein 36g/Carbs 2g/Fat 25g/Fiber 1g

Total Prep & Cook Time: 6 hours 15 minute

Yields: 4 servings

Estimated cost: $8.25

Ingredients:

- Sirloin steak, 2 pounds
- Sesame oil, 2 tablespoons
- Ground ginger, ½ teaspoon
- Sesame seeds, 2 tablespoons
- Soy sauce, ¼ cup
- Keto-appropriate brown sugar, 1/2 cup
- Green onion, chopped, 2
- Minced garlic, 2 tablespoons
- Water, ¼ cup
- Red pepper flakes, ¼ teaspoon

Method:

1. Slice the meat into thin strips against the grain.
2. Put the beef in a slow cooker.
3. Blend the garlic, red pepper flakes, sesame oil, soy sauce, ginger, water, sugar substitute, and pour over the beef strips.
4. Cook with low heat for six hours.
5. Place the beef in a serving bowl and dribble with the sesame seeds and green onions.

Garlic Butter Salmon

Nutrition facts: Calories 450/Protein 37g/Carbs 6g/Fat 24g/Fiber 3g

Total Prep & Cook Time: 28 minutes

Yields: 4 servings

Estimated cost: $10.25

Ingredients:

- Butter, ¼ cup divided
- Cauliflower florets, 1 pound
- Lemon wedges for serving, if desired
- Minced garlic, 3 tablespoons
- Pepper and salt as need
- Lemon zest, 1 teaspoon
- Parsley, chopped fresh, 2 tablespoons
- Salmon filet, 2 pounds cut in 4 servings

Method:

1. Warm your oven to 400 F.
2. Set two tablespoons of butter on a baking flat and put in the oven while heating to temperature.
3. Blend the lemon zest, parsley, and garlic into the leftover butter after it is melted.
4. Pepper and salt the florets if needed and bake them for ten minutes.
5. Set the salmon on the cookie flat and cook for fourteen minutes.

Sausage Alfredo

Nutrition facts: Calories 583/Protein 16g/Carbs 6g/Fat 52g/Fiber 1g

Total Prep & Cook Time: 32 minutes

Yields: 4 servings

Estimated cost: $6.75

Ingredients:

- Ground hot Italian sausage, 12 ounces
- Minced garlic, 3 tablespoons
- Frozen zucchini noodles, 2 pounds thawed
- Heavy whipping cream, 1 cup
- Butter, 2 tablespoons
- Pepper and salt as need
- Freshly grated parmesan cheese, ½ cup

Method:

1. Fry the sausage for seven to eight minutes and remove it from the skillet.
2. Melt the butter in the leftover fat from the sausage.
3. Fry the garlic for three minutes.
4. Cream in the heavy cream and simmer for eight minutes.
5. Blend in the parmesan cheese and any salt and pepper you want.
6. Stir in the sausage along with the zucchini noodles.

Caprese Chicken

Nutrition facts: Calories 325/Protein 36g/Carbs 2g/Fat 19g/Fiber 1g

Total Prep & Cook Time: 45 minutes

Yields: 4 servings

Estimated cost: $7.25

Ingredients:

- Chopped fresh basil, ¼ cup
- Tomato, 1 medium-sized sliced into 6 slices
- Fresh mozzarella slices, 6
- Black pepper, ½ teaspoon
- Salt, ¼ teaspoon
- Boneless skinless chicken thighs, 6
- Avocado oil, 2 tablespoons

Method:

1. Warm your oven to 375 F.
2. Pepper and salt the chicken and fry in oil for three minutes on each side.
3. Grease a rectangular baking dish.
4. Lay the seared chicken thighs in the baking dish.
5. Put on each thigh a slice of cheese and a tomato slice and bake for twenty-five minutes.
6. Sprinkle the baked chicken with fresh basil.

Shrimp and Sausage Skillet

Nutrition facts: Calories 330/Protein 32/Carbs 7/Fat 23g/Fiber 3g

Total Prep & Cook Time: 25 minutes

Yields: 4 servings

Estimated cost: $8.25

Ingredients:

- Avocado oil, ¼ cup
- Cajun seasoning, 1 teaspoon
- Minced jalapeno, 1
- Pepper and salt as need
- Peeled and deveined Shrimp, 1 pound
- Red bell pepper, cleaned and sliced thinly
- Minced garlic, 1 tablespoon
- Chicken sausage links, 12 ounces chunked
- Cut green beans, ½ pound

Method:

1. Cook the Shrimp for two minutes in two tablespoons of the avocado oil.
2. Flip the Shrimp over and season, then cook for two more minutes and remove.
3. Fry the sausage for three to five minutes in the leftover oil.
4. Put in the jalapeno and garlic and cook for three minutes.
5. Mix in the beans and bell pepper and fry for five to ten minutes, just until they feel tender.
6. Stir the Shrimp back in and serve.

Creamy Spinach Feta Chicken

Nutrition facts: Calories 338/Protein 21g/Carbs 3g/Fat 27g/Fiber 1g

Total Prep & Cook Time: 40 minutes

Yields: 6 servings

Estimated cost: $6.95

Ingredients:

- Bacon slices, 6 chopped
- Butter, 1 tablespoon
- Crumbled feta cheese, ½ cup
- Minced garlic, 2 tablespoons
- Boneless skinless chicken thighs, 6
- Grated parmesan cheese, ½ cup
- Black pepper, 1 teaspoon
- Heavy cream, 1 cup
- Salt, ½ teaspoon
- Baby spinach, 1 cup

Method:

1. Fry the bacon crispy, then take the bacon to a paper towel, leaving the skillet's bacon fat.
2. Pepper and salt the chicken and fry them for five minutes on each side and remove.
3. Melt the butter into the leftover fat, cook the minced garlic for one minute, and then stir in the spinach until it wilts.
4. Stir in the parmesan and the heavy cream until it thickens, three to four minutes.
5. Put the chopped bacon back in the pan.

6. Stir in the chicken and cover with the skillet ingredients.
7. Put the ingredients of the skillet into a serving bowl and sprinkle with the crumbled feta cheese.

Brussels sprouts and Asian Shrimp

Nutrition facts: Calories 298/Protein 31g/Carbs 9g/Fat 10g/Fiber 3g

Total Prep & Cook Time: 55 minutes

Yields: 4 servings

Estimated cost: $6.95

Ingredients:

- Salt, ½ teaspoon
- Rice vinegar, 2 tablespoons
- Olive oil, 2 tablespoons
- Sesame oil, 1 tablespoon
- Black pepper, 1 teaspoon
- Soy sauce, 1/3 cup
- Garlic powder, ½ teaspoon
- Peeled and deveined jumbo frozen Shrimp, 1 pound thawed
- Trimmed and sliced Brussels sprouts, 1 pound
- Agave nectar, 2 teaspoons
- Stevia, 2 tablespoons

Method:

1. Heat your oven to 400 F.
2. Grease a baking sheet.
3. Blend the garlic powder, sesame oil, agave nectar, stevia, rice vinegar, and soy sauce for the glaze.
4. Dry the shrimp and coat with half of the glaze mixture.
5. Toss the Brussels sprout halves with pepper, olive oil, and salt, spread them on the baking flat, and cook for fifteen minutes.

6. Set the shrimp on the baking flat and cook for ten more minutes.
7. Put the Shrimp and sprouts in a serving bowl and coat with the leftover glaze.

Pork Stir Fry

Nutrition facts: Calories 399/Protein 20g/Carbs 7g/Fat 30g/Fiber 1g

Total Prep & Cook Time: 35 minutes

Yields: 4 servings

Estimated cost: $6.55

Ingredients:

- Rice wine vinegar, 2 tablespoons
- Chopped fresh ginger root, 2 teaspoons
- Garlic, minced, 2 tablespoons
- Onion, minced, ½ cup
- Chili garlic sauce, 1 tablespoon
- Soy sauce, 2 tablespoons
- Green bean chunks, ½ pound
- Coconut oil, 2 tablespoons
- Ground pork, 1 pound

Method:

1. Stir together the garlic sauce, soy sauce, and rice wine vinegar and set off to the side.
2. Fry the green beans in one tablespoon of oil for two to three minutes, stirring often, then remove and drain.
3. Cook the onion, ginger root, and garlic in the leftover oil for three minutes.
4. Mix in the ground pork and cook until done, five to six minutes.
5. Blend in the sauce mix, then stir in the green beans and serve.

Cheesy Cabbage and Smoked Sausage

Nutrition facts: Calories 334/Protein 16g/Carbs 8g/Fat 25g/Fiber 4g

Total Prep & Cook Time: 55 minutes

Yields: 8 servings

Estimated cost: $5.95

Ingredients:

- Olive oil, 2 tablespoons
- Black pepper, 1 teaspoon
- Garlic, minced, 3 tablespoons
- Parsley, chopped fresh, ¼ cup
- Salt, ½ teaspoon
- Butter, 2 tablespoons
- Onion, diced, 1 cup
- Green cabbage, 1 head shredded
- Tomatoes diced with juice, 1 14-ounce can
- Mozzarella cheese, shredded, 1 ½ cups
- Chopped yellow bell pepper, 1
- Smoked sausage, 14 ounces sliced thinly
- Tomatoes crushed with juice, 1 14-ounce can

Method:

1. Warm your oven to 425 F.
2. Put the butter and oil into a skillet.
3. Fry the onion, cabbage, pepper, garlic, bell pepper, and salt for ten minutes, stirring often.
4. Add in the sausage and tomatoes and cook for ten more minutes.

5. Grease an eight-inch baking dish.
6. Add the ingredients from the skillet to the baking dish and smother with the shredded cheese.
7. Bake for fifteen minutes and top with the parsley to serve.

Garlic Pork Tenderloin

Nutrition facts: Calories 395/Protein 43g/Carbs 9g/Fat 18g/Fiber 4g

Total Prep & Cook Time: 50 minutes

Yields: 6 servings

Estimated cost: $8.50

Ingredients:

- Salt, ½ teaspoon
- Keto brown sugar, ¼ cup
- Leafy greens, 3 cups
- Avocado oil, ¼ cup
- Italian seasoning, 1 teaspoon
- Minced garlic, 4 tablespoons
- Black pepper, 1 teaspoon
- Pork tenderloin, 2 pounds
- Dijon mustard, 2 teaspoons

Method:

1. Warm your oven to 425 F.
2. Wipe the tenderloin dry and pepper and salt it.
3. Grease a rectangular baking dish and set the tenderloin in it.
4. Blend the Italian seasoning, mustard, garlic, sugar, and oil and coat the tenderloin with this mixture.
5. Bake the meat for twenty-five minutes and let stand for ten minutes before slicing.
6. Serve with a leafy green salad.

Spanish Style Cauliflower Rice

Nutrition facts: Calories 352/Protein 29g/Carbs 7g/Fat 22g/Fiber 2g

Total Prep & Cook Time: 25 minutes

Yields: 6 servings

Estimated cost: $5.50

Ingredients:

- Diced onion, ¼ cup
- Sharp cheddar cheese, shredded, 1 ½ cups
- Red bell pepper, diced, ½ cup
- Chicken broth, ½ cup
- Diced tomatoes, 1 cup
- Ground beef, 1 pound
- Frozen cauliflower rice, 12 ounces thawed and drained
- Taco seasoning, 3 tablespoons

Method:

1. Cook the ground beef until almost done, breaking into crumbles as you stir.
2. Put in the onion and pepper and cook five more minutes.
3. Blend in the taco seasoning, broth, cauliflower rice, and tomatoes and cook for ten more minutes.
4. Dribble the cheese on the mixture and let it sit for the cheese to melt, then serve.

Lemon Dill Tuna Cakes

Nutrition facts per pattie: Calories 215/Protein 22g/Carbs 2g/Fat 14g/Fiber 1g

Total Prep & Cook Time: 25 minutes

Yields: 8 patties

Estimated cost: $4.95

Ingredients:

- Chopped green onion, 2
- Salt, ½ teaspoon
- Chopped fresh dill, 3 tablespoons
- Lemon zest, 1 tablespoon
- Avocado oil, 2 tablespoons
- Drained tuna in oil, 4 5-ounce cans
- Black pepper, ½ teaspoon
- Lemon juice, 1 tablespoon
- Egg, 1
- Mayonnaise, ¼ cup
- Almond flour, 1/3 cup

Method:

1. Blend everything except the avocado oil until well mixed.
2. Form the mixture into eight patties that are about three-fourths inches thick.
3. Fry the patties in the avocado oil for five minutes on each side, turning over carefully.
4. Serve the patties with lemon juice and mayonnaise if desired.

Chapter 7: Sauces and Dressings

Sauces and dressings bought in the grocery store are full of added sugar and preservatives you do not want in your keto-friendly foods. These are simple to make at home with fresh ingredients that you can make your own to compliment your meal creations.

Hummus

Nutrition facts for the quarter cup: Calories 427/Protein 5g/Carbs 4g/Fat 41g/Fiber 5g

Total Prep & Cook Time: 15 minutes

Yields: 1 cup

Estimated cost: $3.15

Ingredients:

- Black pepper, ½ teaspoon
- Freshly chopped cilantro, ½ cup
- Ripe avocados, 3
- Minced garlic, 1 tablespoon
- Cumin, ground, ½ teaspoon
- Salt, 1/4 teaspoon
- Sunflower seeds, ¼ cup
- Lime juice, 2 tablespoons
- Avocado oil, ½ cup
- Tahini, ¼ cup

Method:

1. Wipe off the skin of the avocados and peel them.
2. Put the avocado flesh into your blender.
3. Put in the remainder of the ingredients and blend until creamy smooth.

Spicy Pimiento Cheese Spread

Nutrition facts for the quarter cup: Calories 248/Protein 7g/Carbs 1g/Fat 24g/Fiber 1g

Total Prep & Cook Time: 1 hour 15 minutes

Yields: 1 cup

Estimated cost: $2.25

Ingredients:

- Cayenne pepper, 1/8 teaspoon
- Chili powder, 1 teaspoon
- Cheese, shredded cheddar, ½ cup
- Paprika, 1 teaspoon
- Mayonnaise, 1/3 cup
- Finely chopped pimientos, 4 tablespoons
- Dijon mustard, 1 tablespoon

Method:

1. Cream the mayonnaise, mustard, and shredded cheese.
2. Add in the chili powder, paprika, and cayenne pepper.
3. Fold in the pimientos just until blended.
4. Chill this mixture for one hour before serving.

Salsa Dressing

Nutrition facts for the quarter cup: Calories 200/Protein 1g/Carbs 2g/Fat 21g/Fiber 6g

Total Prep & Cook Time: 1 hour 15 minutes

Yields: 1 cup

Estimated cost: $2.50

Ingredients:

- Diced tomatoes, ½ cup
- Sour cream, 2 tablespoons
- Garlic, minced, 1 tablespoon
- Apple cider vinegar, 3 tablespoons
- Olive oil, ¼ cup
- Mayonnaise, 4 tablespoons
- Chili powder, 1 teaspoon

Method:

1. Cream the olive oil, sour cream, vinegar, and mayonnaise.
2. Mix in the diced tomatoes, chili powder, and minced garlic.
3. Chill the dressing for one hour before serving.

Barbeque Sauce

Nutrition facts: Calories 13/Protein 0g/Carbs 2g/Fat 2g/Fiber 1g

Total Prep & Cook Time: 40 minutes

Yields: 12 servings

Estimated cost: $3.25

Ingredients:

- Chili powder, 1 tablespoon
- Dijon mustard, 2 tablespoons
- Liquid smoke, 2 teaspoons
- Agave nectar, 1 teaspoon
- Salt, 1 teaspoon
- Apple cider vinegar, 2 tablespoons
- Garlic powder, ½ teaspoon
- Worcestershire sauce, 2 tablespoons
- Canned tomato sauce, 1 8-ounce can
- Onion powder, 1 tablespoon

Method:

1. Mix everything well in a saucepan.
2. Boil the mixture, and then simmer for thirty minutes.

Ranch Dressing

Nutrition facts for the quarter cup: Calories 241/Protein 1g/Carbs 1g/Fat 26g/Fiber 0g

Total Prep & Cook Time: 1 hour 10 minutes

Yields: 1 cup

Estimated cost: $4.15

Ingredients:

- Mayonnaise, 1 cup
- Almond milk, ½ cup
- Sour cream, ½ cup
- Ranch seasoning powder, 2 tablespoons

Method:

1. Mix everything well and refrigerate.
2. Let the dressing chill for one hour before serving.

Mayonnaise

Nutrition facts for quarter cup: Calories 511/Protein 1 gram/Carbs 0g/Fat 57g/Fiber 0g

Total Prep & Cook Time: 30 minutes

Yields: 1 ¼ cup

Estimated cost: $3.75

Ingredients:

- Lemon juice, 3 teaspoons
- Olive oil, 1 cup
- Dijon mustard, 1 tablespoon
- Room temperature egg yolk, 1

Method:

1. Cream the egg yolk and mustard.
2. Continue stirring and pouring in the oil to blend well.
3. Add in the lemon juice.
4. Let the mixture thicken before using.

Strawberry Jam

Nutrition facts for one tablespoon: Calories 57/Protein 1g/Carbs 1g/Fat 0g/Fiber 6g

Total Prep & Cook Time: 45 minutes

Yields: 1 ½ cup

Estimated cost: $5.25

Ingredients:

- Diced strawberries, 1 cup
- Water, ¼ cup
- Gelatin powder, ¾ teaspoon
- Agave nectar, ¼ cup
- Lemon juice, 2 tablespoon

Method:

1. Dribble the gelatin on the lemon juice in a small bowl and let it sit until it becomes thick.
2. Put the stevia, strawberries, and water on the stove.
3. Simmer for twenty minutes.
4. Slice up the lemon juice gelatin mixture and stir it into the strawberry mixture on the stove until it has dissolved.
5. Cool jam to room temperature.
6. Scoop the jam into a jar or bowl and keep refrigerated.
7. This jam can also be made with any other type of berry.

Blue Cheese Dressing

Nutrition facts for one-quarter cup: Calories 477/Protein 10g/Carbs 4g/Fat 47g/Fiber 0g

Total Prep & Cook Time: 1 hour 15 minutes

Yields: 2 cups

Estimated cost: $4.75

Ingredients:

- Greek yogurt, ¾ cup
- Black pepper, 1 teaspoon
- Salt, 1 teaspoon
- Parsley, chopped fresh, 2 tablespoons
- Heavy whipping cream, ½ cup
- Blue cheese, ½ cup
- Mayonnaise, ½ cup

Method:

1. Chop up the blue cheese into crumbles in a large bowl.
2. Blend in the yogurt, mayonnaise, and heavy cream.
3. Add in the pepper, salt, and parsley.
4. Let the dressing refrigerate for one hour before using.

Guacamole

Nutrition facts for the one-quarter cup: Calories 238/Protein 3g/Carbs 5g/Fat 22g/Fiber 3g

Total Prep & Cook Time: 2 hours 20 minutes

Yields: 2 cups

Estimated cost: $5.95

Ingredients:

- Black pepper, 1 teaspoon
- Olive oil, 2 tablespoons
- Salt, ½ teaspoon
- Chopped white onion, ¼ cup
- Ripe avocado, 2
- Minced garlic, 1 tablespoon
- Chopped fresh cilantro, 4 tablespoons
- Diced tomato, ¼ cup
- Lime juice, 2 tablespoons

Method:

1. Wipe off the avocados' skin and peel them, discarding the peel and the pit.
2. In a mixing bowl, mash the pulp of the avocado.
3. Stir in the remainder of the ingredients and let the guacamole sit for two hours before serving.

Caesar Dressing

Nutrition facts for the one-quarter cup: Calories 298/Protein 6g/Carbs 1g/Fat 31g/Fiber 1g

Total Prep & Cook Time: 1 hour 15 minutes

Yields: 1 cup

Estimated cost: $5.15

Ingredients:

- Grated parmesan cheese, ¼ cup
- Minced garlic, 1 teaspoon
- Chopped anchovies or anchovy paste, 1 tablespoon
- Black pepper, ½ tablespoon
- Dijon mustard, 1 tablespoon
- Lemon juice, 1 tablespoon
- Salt, ½ teaspoon
- Apple cider vinegar, 1 teaspoon
- Olive oil, ½ cup

Method:

1. Mix everything well.
2. Use a few drops of water if the dressing is too thick.
3. Refrigerate the dressing for one hour before using.

Chapter 8: Dessert Recipes

Chocolate Walnut Torte

Nutrition facts: Calories 343/Protein 10g/Carbs 8g/Fat 31g/Fiber 6g

Total Prep & Cook Time: 1 hour 15 minutes

Yields: 12 servings

Estimated cost: $10.25

Ingredients:

FOR THE GLAZE

- Chopped walnut pieces, 1/3 cup
- Chopped sugar-free dark chocolate, 3 ounces
- Heavy whipping cream, ½ cup

FOR THE TORTE

- Almond milk, ½ cup
- Vanilla extract, 1 teaspoon
- Eggs, 5
- Unsweetened chocolate, 4 ounces
- Butter, ½ cup
- Salt, ¼ teaspoon
- Baking powder, ½ teaspoon
- Cocoa powder, ¼ cup
- Stevia, ¾ cup
- Chopped walnuts, 1 ½ cup

Method:

1. Warm your oven to 325 F.
2. Oil a nine-inch round baking pan.
3. Combine the salt, baking powder, cocoa powder, sweetener, and chopped walnuts for the torte.
4. Melt the butter and chocolate until creamy, then take the pan from the heat.
5. Blend in the vanilla extract, eggs, and almond milk.
6. Blend the chocolate mixture with the powdered cocoa mixture.
7. Bake for thirty minutes. Cool the cake for thirty minutes in the pan before removing it.
8. To make the glaze, heat the cream until it simmers. Then take the pan off the heat.
9. Put in the chocolate and let it sit for five minutes to melt, then blend everything smooth.
10. Dribble the glaze over the cake and sprinkle on the chopped walnuts.

Chewy Molasses Ginger Cookies

Nutrition facts: Calories 157/Protein 5g/Carbs 4g/Fat 13g/Fiber 2g
Total Prep & Cook Time: 34 minutes
Yields: 40 cookies (20 servings)
Estimated cost: $7.35

Ingredients:

- Almond Flour, 2 cups
- Butter, 1/2 cup at room temperature
- Baking soda, ½ teaspoon
- Vanilla extract, ½ teaspoon
- Gelatin powder, 2 tablespoons
- Agave nectar, 2 teaspoons
- Ground cloves, ¼ teaspoon
- Ground ginger, 1 tablespoon
- Eggs, 2 at room temperature
- Cinnamon, 1 teaspoon
- Sugar replacement, 1 cup
- Cashew or almond butter, ½ cup

Method:

1. Warm your oven to 325 F.
2. Cover two oven flats with silicone liners or parchment.
3. Blend the ginger, cinnamon, cloves, gelatin, baking soda, and almond flour.
4. In a different bowl, cream together the vanilla extract, eggs, sweetener, butter, and almond butter. Put the butter mixture in the flour mixture and stir well.
5. Roll the batter into balls one inch across and set on the baking flats two inches apart.
6. Bake the cookies for twelve minutes.

Lemon Cheesecake Bars

Nutrition facts: Calories 190/Protein 4g/Carbs 3g/Fat 17g/Fiber 1g
Total Prep & Cook Time: 3 hours 10 minutes
Yields: 16 bars (16 servings)
Estimated cost: $6.45

Ingredients:

- FOR THE FILLING
    - Eggs, 2
    - Heavy whipping cream, 2 tablespoons
    - Lemon juice, 3 tablespoons
    - Lemon zest, 2 teaspoons
    - Powdered sugar substitute, ½ cup
    - Softened cream cheese, 16 ounces

- FOR THE CRUST
    - Melted butter, ¼ cup
    - Salt, ¼ teaspoon
    - Sugar substitute, ¼ cup
    - Almond flour, 1 ¼ cups

Method:

1. Warm your oven to 325 F.
2. Mix the salt, sweetener, and almond flour for the crust, then stir in the melted butter.
3. Grease an eight-inch baking pan.
4. Push the crust into the greased pan and cook for ten minutes.
5. Lower the temperature of the oven to 275 F.
6. Cream the filling cheesecake with the heavy cream, lemon juice, lemon zest, and sweetener until smooth.
7. Blend in the eggs gently just until mixed.

8. Put the filling mixture over the prebaked crust and smooth.
9. Bake the bars for forty minutes.
10. Cool for thirty minutes at room temperature, then chill the bars for two hours before slicing.

No Churn Strawberry Ice Cream

Nutrition facts: Calories 202/Protein 2g/Carbs 4g/Fat 19g/Fiber 1g
Total Prep & Cook Time: 25 minutes
Yields: 10 servings
Estimated cost: $6.25

Ingredients:

- Fresh strawberries, 2 cups
- Sour cream, 1 ½ cups
- Powdered sugar substitute, 1/3 cup
- Vanilla extract, 1 teaspoon
- Xylitol, ¼ cup
- Heavy whipping cream, 1 ½ cup

Method:

1. Blend the xylitol and fresh strawberries until almost wholly pureed.
2. Stir together the strawberry puree with the vanilla extract and sour cream.
3. In another bowl, whip the heavy cream and the powdered sugar substitute until you form stiff peaks when the beaters are raised.
4. Mix the whipped cream gently into the strawberry mixture until just mixed.
5. Freeze the mixture for six hours before serving.

Chocolate Mousse Pie

Nutrition facts: Calories 321/Protein 6g/Carbs 5g/Fat 29g/Fiber 4g
Total Prep & Cook Time: 1 hour
Yields: 12 servings
Estimated cost: $8.15

Ingredients:

- FOR THE MOUSSE
  - Vanilla extract, ½ teaspoon
  - Heavy whipping cream, 1 1/2 cup
  - Salt 1/8 teaspoon
  - Cream of tartar, ¼ teaspoon
  - Powdered sugar substitute, ½ cup divided
  - Egg whites, 4
  - Butter, 1 tablespoon
  - Chopped unsweetened chocolate, 4 ounces

- FOR THE CRUST
  - Melted butter, ¼ cup
  - Salt, ¼ teaspoon
  - Powdered sugar substitute, ¼ cup
  - Cocoa powder, ¼ cup
  - Almond flour, 1 ¼ cup

- FOR THE TOPPING
  - Powdered sugar substitute, 2 tablespoons
  - Heavy whipping cream, ½ cup

Method:

1. Warm your oven to 350 F.

2. Grease a nine-inch round glass baking pan.
3. Make the crust by mixing the salt, sweetener, cocoa powder, and almond flour, then mix in the melted butter.
4. Push this mixture into the bottom and sides of the greased glass baking dish.
5. Bake the crust for twelve minutes.
6. Microwave the chocolate and butter for the mousse for thirty seconds at a time until they are melted and mixed.
7. Whip the egg whites with one-fourth cup of the powdered sweetener and microwave for one minute.
8. Put in the salt with the cream of tartar and beat the eggs until they form stiff peaks.
9. Mix the vanilla and leftover powdered sugar substitute into the whipping cream and beat this until it makes soft peaks.
10. Fold into the egg whites the melted chocolate.
11. Fold the chocolate and egg whites into the whipping cream.
12. Spread this mixture over the cooked crust and chill the mousse for four hours.
13. After four hours, blend the powdered sugar substitute and heavy whipping cream for the topping and spread it over the mousse.

Peppermint Bark

Nutrition facts: Calories 131/Protein 1g/Carbs 3g/Fat 14g/Fiber 2g
Total Prep & Cook Time: 35 minutes
Yields: 12 servings
Estimated cost: $7.90

Ingredients:

- FOR THE DARK CHOCOLATE LAYER
  - Peppermint extract, ½ teaspoon
  - Cocoa butter, ½ ounce
  - Chopped unsweetened dark chocolate, 4 ounces

- FOR THE WHITE CHOCOLATE LAYER
  - Peppermint extract, ½ teaspoon
  - Powdered sugar substitute, 3 tablespoons
  - Coconut oil, ¼ cup
  - Cocoa butter, 2 ounces

1. Make the dark chocolate layer by microwaving the cocoa butter and chopped chocolate in thirty-second intervals until stirred smoothly.
2. Grease an eight-inch baking dish and pour in the dark chocolate layer.
3. Freeze the chocolate layer for thirty minutes.
4. Make the white chocolate layer by microwaving the coconut oil and cocoa butter in thirty-second intervals until stirred smooth.
5. Spread the layer of white chocolate over the dark chocolate layer and freeze for thirty minutes.
6. Store the peppermint bark in the refrigerator.

Coconut Milk Chocolate Pudding

Nutrition facts: Calories 228/Protein 4g/Carbs 4g/Fat 23g/Fiber 2g
Total Prep & Cook Time: 22 minutes
Yields: 6 servings
Estimated cost: $6.80

Ingredients:

- Coconut milk, 1 13 to 14 ounce can
- Sugar substitute, 1/3 cup
- Avocado oil, 3 tablespoons
- Dark cocoa powder, 1/3 cup
- Egg yolks, 3
- Xanthan gum, ¼ teaspoon
- Vanilla extract, ½ teaspoon

Method:

1. Simmer the sugar substitute and coconut milk for five minutes.
2. Stir in the beaten egg yolks.
3. Add in the xanthan gum and cocoa powder and simmer for five more minutes.
4. Take the pan off the heat and put in the vanilla and avocado oil, stirring until smooth.
5. Spoon the pudding into six dessert glasses and refrigerate for thirty minutes.

Fudgy Brownies

Nutrition facts: Calories 110/Protein 3g/Carbs 4g/Fat 10g/Fiber 3g
Total Prep & Cook Time: 40 minutes
Yields: 16 servings
Estimated cost: $6.95

Ingredients:

- Melted butter, ½ cup
- Chocolate chips, dark, sugar-free, 1/3 cup
- Vanilla extract, ½ teaspoon
- Almond flour, ½ cup
- Unsweetened cocoa powder, 1/3 cup
- Stevia, 2/3 cup
- Water, ¼ cup (if needed)
- Eggs, 3
- Salt, ¼ teaspoon
- Baking powder, ½ cup
- Gelatin powder, 1 tablespoon

Method:

1. Heat your oven to 350 F.
2. Grease an eight-inch baking dish.
3. Cream together the vanilla extract, eggs, sweetener, and butter until creamy.
4. Stir in the baking powder, cocoa powder, salt, gelatin, and almond flour until the batter is smooth.
5. Use water as needed.
6. Push the batter in the greased baking dish and cook the brownies for twenty minutes.

Conclusion

You have now reached the end of *Keto Diet for Dummies 2021*. Hopefully, you found this book interesting and informative, with all of the information you need to begin your keto lifestyle.

The next step is to begin your journey. As you have seen in this cookbook, keto eating is not boring. You can eat fresh foods and flavorful foods that will make you happy and healthy at the same time. You can eat real foods and eat enough food to keep you feeling full. One of the biggest problems with most diet plans is that the calories are so restricted that people quit before seeing any real results. But with the keto diet, you will eat enough food to keep you satisfied. This will help you avoid the foods you do not need. The foods you will eat will be so enjoyable you will never miss the sugar and processed foods.

Since you will be eating enough food to keep your body satisfied, you will soon lose the desire to overeat. The nutrition of the keto diet will provide you with all of the nutrients you need to succeed. Try the recipes in this book, and then begin creating your meal plans.

Hopefully, this book was useful to you in many ways, and a review on Amazon is always appreciated!

Made in the USA
Middletown, DE
13 June 2021